5-8

MANUAL
for STAGE ONE *of the*
Reading Progress Tests

(for use with the Literacy Baseline and Reading Progress Tests 1 and 2)

Denis Vincent,
Mary Crumpler
and Mike de la Mare

Hodder & Stoughton
A MEMBER OF THE HODDER HEADLINE GROUP

About this manual

This manual gives instructions for administering, marking and interpreting the results of Stage One of the Reading Progress Tests series:

- Literacy Baseline

- Reading Progress Test 1

- Reading Progress Test 2.

A separate manual is provided for use with Stage Two of the series, covering Reading Progress Tests 3 to 6.

Acknowledgements

The authors have been unable to trace the owner of the copyright for *Karen doesn't like a cone*, in RPT1, but would be pleased to make appropriate acknowledgement in future editions of this Manual.

ISBN 0 340 66359 6
First published 1996: reprinted (with amendments) 1996.

Impression number 10 9
Year 2005, 2004, 2003, 2002, 2001, 2000

Copyright © 1996 Hodder & Stoughton Ltd

All rights reserved. No part of this publication may be reproduced or transmitted in any form or by any means, electronic or mechanical, including photocopying recording or any information storage and retrieval system, without permission in writing from the publisher. *This publication is excluded from the reprographic licensing scheme administered by the Copyright Licensing Agency Ltd.*

Printed in Great Britain for Hodder & Stoughton Educational, the educational publishing division of Hodder Headline Plc, 338 Euston Road, London, NW1 3BH, by Hobbs The Printers, Totton, Hampshire

Contents

Introduction	**5**
The Reading Progress Tests series	5
Literacy Baseline	6
RPT1 and RPT2	7
Using the tests to measure progress	**9**
Scheduling of tests	9
Using the results	10
Factors affecting progress	10
Screening with the Literacy Baseline	**12**
Administration	**13**
Literacy Baseline	13
RPT1	21
RPT2	24
Marking	**27**
Literacy Baseline	27
RPT1	28
RPT2	29
Using and interpreting the conversion tables	**30**
Introduction	30
Standardised scores	30
Reading ages	31
Ability scale scores	32
Progress scores	32
Case studies	34
Conversion tables	**36**
Literacy Baseline	36
RPT1	38
RPT2	40
Progress	42
Development and standardisation	**45**
Literacy Baseline	45
RPT1 and RPT2	45
Reliability	46
Validity	47
Reading progress analysis sheet	**48**

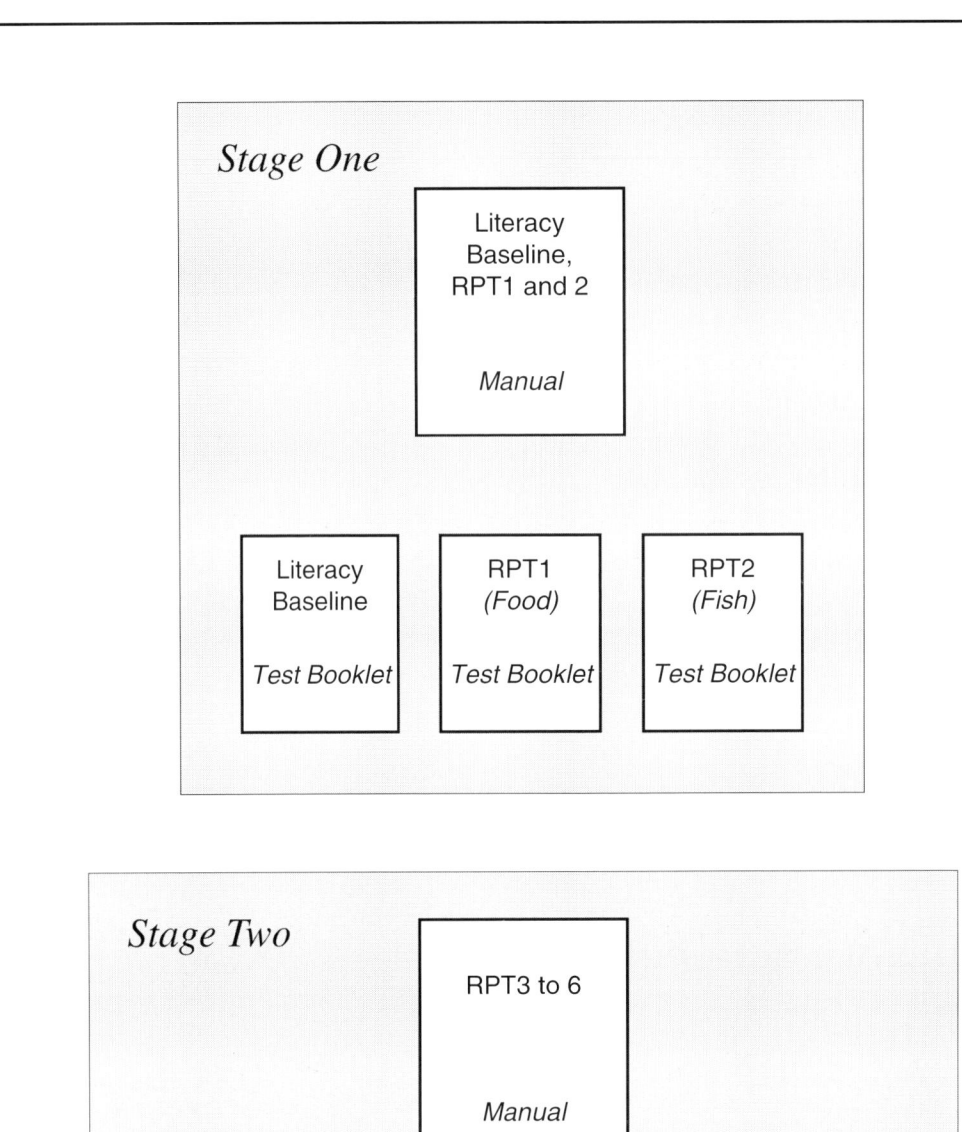

Introduction

The Reading Progress Tests series

The Reading Progress Tests are a series of seven tests for ages 5 to 11. They comprise a Literacy Baseline test (of pre-reading and early reading skills) and six group tests of reading comprehension (Reading Progress Test 1 to Reading Progress Test 6, corresponding to Years 1 to 6 in England and Wales). The series was developed by the East London Assessment Group at the University of East London on behalf of the publishers, Hodder & Stoughton Educational.

The tests provide a continuous measure of individual and group progress in reading throughout the Primary years, which is at once thorough and relatively undemanding in terms of time. They are objectively marked and Reading Progress Tests 1 to 6 maintain a common question format across levels.

Each of the tests except the Literacy Baseline is written around a theme.

Test	Title	Theme
Reading Progress Test 1 (RPT1)		Food
Reading Progress Test 2 (RPT2)		Fish
Reading Progress Test 3 (RPT3)	*Squawk!*	Parrots
Reading Progress Test 4 (RPT4)	*Smell!*	Noses and the sense of smell
Reading Progress Test 5 (RPT5)	*Tails*	Tails
Reading Progress Test 6 (RPT6)	*What is it?*	Mysteries

These themes were chosen to allow interesting, entertaining and varied reading material to be used, so that children would be as motivated as possible when working on the test. Wherever appropriate, the material mirrors the sort of reading a child is likely to encounter in the normal course of events at home or at school.

Each test has conventional cross-sectional norms which give standardised scores and reading ages, as well as ability scale scores. These norms are based on representative samples of children in schools throughout England and Wales. More details are given on pages 45 to 47.

In addition, progress norms have been established, by re-testing these samples of children with the *next* test in the series. These norms enable the teacher to judge to what extent children are making normal progress or are progressing at a rate which is greater or less than is typical. The Reading Progress Tests are the first published standardised group reading comprehension tests available to UK teachers to present norms in this form.

Introduction

The complete series is structured as two stages. *Stage One* is made up of the Literacy Baseline test and Reading Progress Tests 1 and 2, and is designed for use with pupils aged 5 to 7 (Key Stage One of the national curriculum for England and Wales).

Stage Two comprises Reading Progress Tests 3 to 6, and is designed for use with pupils aged 7 to 11 (Key Stage Two of the national curriculum for England and Wales).

To assist the teacher, there is, for each stage, a manual providing instructions on administration, marking and interpretation. For each test in Stage One, pupils are provided with a single test booklet; in Stage Two there are separate Reading Broadsheets (which are re-usable) and test booklets. The structure of the series is shown on page 4.

Literacy Baseline

The Literacy Baseline test is intended for use with children during the first term of their first year of compulsory schooling.

It has three purposes:

- to provide a 'baseline' from which to measure subsequent progress;
- to contribute to screening procedures designed to identify children likely to face difficulties with the development of early reading skills;
- to provide a means of appraising children's early literacy development.

It is generally agreed that for children of this age the best predictor of their later reading skills is how well they already read and spell. A major part of the Literacy Baseline is therefore a series of simple tasks designed to assess existing reading and spelling ability.

Research has shown, however, a number of other abilities which are also associated with later reading development. These include:

- the identification of initial sounds in spoken words (phonological awareness);
- the identification of rhymes in spoken words (phonological awareness);
- familiarity with literacy concepts (such as knowing which words on the cover of a book are likely to give the name of the book, or which is the first word in a line of print);
- knowledge of letter names;
- knowledge of letter sounds.

Simple tests of these abilities have also therefore been included in the Literacy Baseline. Their inclusion means that the test can be a useful predictor of later reading development even for those children who have yet to acquire rudimentary literacy skills.

Children answer questions in the Literacy Baseline by making a mark (or in the Spelling section, writing) in their test booklet. This means that, unlike many of the tests used by researchers, this test need not be administered individually (although this is likely to be necessary in certain instances). Trials showed that it is often possible to administer the test successfully with groups of between three and eight children.

The test is untimed, but can normally be administered in about 20 minutes. The pace is set by the teacher, who will need to ensure that all the children are given time to answer each question.

RPT1 and RPT2

RPT1 and RPT2 are group tests of reading comprehension intended for use, towards the end of the school year, with children in the age range 5 to 6 and 6 to 7, respectively.

They have two main purposes:

- to allow a standardised assessment of a child's reading comprehension;

- to monitor a child's progress in reading comprehension from one assessment point to the next, by comparing it to the progress made by other children in the same age-group.

Both tests are made up of three main types of comprehension question:

- identifying the meaning of individual words;

- selecting the right answer from a number of choices after reading a short story, non-fiction passage or poem;

- choosing, or supplying, missing words in a short story or non-fiction passage.

Except for some questions of the last type, the questions do not require children to write their answers. This means that the tests:

- are able to measure effectively children's reading comprehension even where their writing skills may be limited;

- are relatively quick to administer;

- are quick and easy to mark, and do not require subjective judgements on the part of the marker.

Questions relating to continuous texts cover inferential as well as literal comprehension.

The tests are untimed, and children work through them at their own pace after an initial explanation by the teacher. In practice, 45-50 minutes is usually sufficient. For convenience of administration, the tests are designed to be used with whole classes of children or with large groups.

Using the tests to measure progress

Individual tests in the series can be used as free-standing tests for the various screening, year-on-year monitoring and grouping purposes for which reading tests are customarily used, at any point during the year. The tests are also suitable for use as part of the educational assessment of an individual reader.

However, the particular value of the series is for assessing the amount of *progress* in reading children make during each year of their primary school careers. The tests can be used either as a classroom tool by individual teachers or more formally as part of an overall LEA or school policy for keeping standards of reading progress under close review.

Scheduling of tests

Progress can be assessed using any pair of tests in order. The full recommended schedule for giving the tests is as follows:

Literacy Baseline:	October of Year 1
RPT1:	June/July of Year 1
RPT2:	June/July of Year 2

(RPT3 to RPT6 may be given in June/July of each subsequent school year.)

The progress norms are based on the above set of intervals. However, to allow some flexibility in the scheduling of the tests the conversion tables on pages 42 to 44 of this Manual have been extended to indicate progress over a range of intervals (thus allowing the use of RPT2 in April, for instance, nine complete months after administering RPT1 in the preceding June).

As well as using an adjacent pair of tests, it is also possible to test selectively. For example, RPT1 could be omitted from the programme so that progress is measured from the Literacy Baseline to RPT2. Also, there is no prior requirement for Literacy Baseline results in order to measure progress between any adjacent pairs of tests later in the series.

Using the results

Results obtained for pairs of tests given at six to twelve month intervals can be used as follows:

- where children are progressing normally or at a higher rate than normal, the tests provide schools and teachers with independent and objective confirmation of this;

- where progress is at less than the normal rate, the tests act as an early warning system which can alert teachers to the need to re-appraise their approach to individual learners or their approach to the teaching of reading more generally;

- where the initial attainment of children is lower than average (as might be indicated by RPT1 scores) or pre-literacy and initial literacy skills are less developed (as might be indicated by the Literacy Baseline), the results of progress testing will indicate to what extent children are making the necessary additional progress to catch up and reach a satisfactory level of reading attainment;

- averaged *class* results can also provide useful pointers (see page 35).

Factors affecting progress

The Reading Progress Tests series allows schools and teachers to monitor and evaluate progress in reading. The tests themselves cannot supply an explanation as to *why* particular children or groups happen to make more or less progress than normal. How far effectiveness of teaching should be balanced against other considerations will depend on the circumstances. The possible reasons for educational failure, apart from quality of teaching, are many. Social and familial factors, health, intelligence, frequency of attendance and behavioural factors have all been identified by research as possible causes. Specific learning difficulty (dyslexia) must also be considered, although questions remain about both its definition and its incidence.

It was not possible to gather comprehensive data on all of these in the course of developing the Reading Progress Tests. However, a short checklist was included in the standardisation of the Literacy Baseline which asked teachers to answer 15 questions about each child (see Figure 1). Each question required a rapid Yes/No judgement. There was also an option to respond 'Not Known' although this was, in fact, rarely used.

All of the matters covered in the checklist are, of course, likely to have some bearing on a child's progress in reading and all those in boldface were significantly correlated, positively or negatively, with RPT1 scores. However, of these, only the questions which are also underlined in Figure 1 made an *additional* contribution (in a multiple regression analysis) to the prediction of RPT1 scores based on the Literacy Baseline results. In fact, this additional contribution to the reliability with which reading scores were predicted, although statistically significant, was modest. This suggests that while factors outside the immediate control of the teachers should not be discounted, the 'entry' level of literacy skills children possess remains the major consideration.

- **Attended nursery school**
- Attended infant reception class

- **Reads at home**
- **Is read to at home**
- **Shows some interest in books/reading**

- English is main language at home
- If no, some English spoken at home
- <u>**Fluent in spoken English**</u>

- **Difficulties with hearing**
- Difficulties with sight
- <u>**Difficulties with speech production**</u>
- **Difficulties with movement/co-ordination**

- <u>**Tends to be inattentive in class**</u>
- <u>**Tends to be restless in class**</u>
- **Tends to be anxious in class**

Teachers responded **yes/no/not known** for each child.

Figure 1. Checklist of questions about children who took the Literacy Baseline.

Screening with the Literacy Baseline

The primary function of the Literacy Baseline is to act as an initial reference point against which subsequent progress can be measured. However, it also identifies children who are entering school with weaker pre-literacy skills and for whom the prognosis of reading progress is less favourable. The results of the research involved in developing the test suggest that a raw score of 15 or less on the Literacy Baseline would be a useful criterion for identifying children who may be in especial need of some form of intervention.

There were 302 children in the Literacy Baseline standardisation sample who answered no more than 15 questions correctly. Of these children, 263 (87 per cent) were unable to answer correctly more than four of the first six simple word comprehension questions in RPT1 when they took it 8-9 months later. These questions are very easy relative to others in the test. Children who are unable to answer four or more correctly may reasonably be regarded as having made very limited progress in initial literacy.

As a screening test for later reading difficulty, the Literacy Baseline resulted in few 'false positives'. In other words, it did not give many false alarms: very few children scoring 15 or less managed to answer more than four of the easy word questions correctly on RPT1. At the same time there were more 'false negatives': just over one third of the children who exceeded the cut-score of 15 on the Literacy Baseline also later failed to answer correctly more than four of the six initial RPT1 questions. In other words, as a screening test the Literacy Baseline will pick out children who are at risk and will make few mistakes in those it identifies, but those are not necessarily the *only* children who may merit concern. This reflects the fact that reading is a multi-faceted skill, and a relative lack of difficulty at one stage of a child's reading development does *not* mean that all subsequent reading development will necessarily be problem-free. It also highlights the need for a reading assessment programme within which reading development is recognised as a dynamic process, with spurts, pauses and perhaps occasional regression, rather than seen as a fixed, static entity.

Although the Literacy Baseline is therefore a useful starting point for screening and intervention, the results show that, as with any reading screening procedure, teachers should not rely on it as a 'once only' assessment. In particular, the reading development of children whose scores lie immediately above the cut-score of 15 should continue to be carefully monitored.

Administration: Literacy Baseline

Group size
Use the test with whatever size of group you feel is most manageable. You may wish to vary the size of the groups depending on the independence of the children concerned. It is suggested that groups of between three and eight children are generally likely to be appropriate, but that some children will need to be tested individually.

Timing
The children work through the test at a pace set by you. This should be relatively brisk, although children should be allowed adequate time to consider their answers. Depending on circumstances, the test is generally likely to be completed within 20 minutes.

It is important that, apart from where there are exceptional circumstances, children attempt all questions. It is recommended that the materials be worked through in a single session.

Preparation
Each child should have a copy of the test booklet and writing materials. There is a question in the test which requires the child to write his/her own first name, so during the test each child's booklet should be identified by just his/her initials.

You will need a copy of the test booklet as well as these instructions.

Test conditions
It is important that the children complete their answers without discussion, collaboration or copying.

Method of answering
Most answers are made by underlining a choice. If necessary, however, children can indicate their answers by pointing, with you or another adult underlining on their behalf. If the children you are working with are more used to indicating their answers by some other means (such as by putting a ring round their chosen answer), rather than by underlining, they may answer in this way. The instructions you give the children will need to be changed accordingly.

Answers may be altered by rubbing or crossing out.

Be as encouraging as possible, but do not give feedback as to whether answers are right or wrong, except in the practice questions. However, where the *method* of answering is wrong – for instance if more than one choice has been underlined, or the child is looking at the wrong set of pictures – remind him or her of how to answer and allow time for an appropriate alteration to be made.

Administration

Question and page numbers

The children's test booklets contain question numbers and page numbers. These are included to make preparation and marking easier for the test administrator. You should **not** refer children to the numbering when working through the test, as this will disadvantage and distract those children who have yet to develop initial number knowledge.

Giving the Literacy Baseline test

In the greater part of the test the questions are presented orally by you, with the children making their answers in the test booklet. The only parts of the test where you do not present each question separately are the reading sections, where it is sufficient to explain the way the questions are answered. Detailed question-by-question instructions are given below, and these should be followed carefully.

Suggested wording for you to use when explaining the questions to the children is given in italics. You do not need to keep to this verbatim – the most important thing is that the children know what they have to do.

Where there are spoken target words, these should be repeated twice, and up to three further times if requested.

Literacy Baseline

Phonological awareness: initial sounds
(Pages 1 and 2)

These questions are to establish the extent to which a child can consciously distinguish the opening sounds of words. All words are read aloud by you – the pictures are memory aids for the children. It is important that you do not separate or unduly emphasise the first sound in the word: say the words in a deliberate but natural manner.

If children are not familiar with the concept of 'odd one out', some preliminary work on this may be necessary, using for instance familiar classroom objects. Avoid using sound discrimination as the basis for this.

Point to the first three pictures on the first page (the child's booklet if you are working individually, your own booklet if you are working with a group). This first question is for practice only.

Say: *Look at these three pictures. The first one's a **bun**, the next one's a **bat**, and the last one's a **tin**.*

Repeat:

(P) **bun   bat   tin**

*You've got to find the odd one out. Can you hear that **bun** and **bat** start with the same sound* (make a 'b' sound). ***Tin*** *starts with a 't' sound. That means **tin** is the odd one out.*

*You must put a line under the odd one out. So put a line under **tin**.*

Check that the question has been completed correctly. If a child has underlined the wrong answer, try to establish where the misunderstanding arises and rectify it. Remember that the purpose is to establish whether the child can detect the difference between the sounds, rather than to train them to detect such differences. When you are satisfied the children understand what they have to do, go on to Question 1.

Remember that the main cue the children have are the words read aloud by you, and that the words need to be read in a natural way.

Point to the three pictures in Question 1 and say:

Now try these. Each time put a line under the odd one out.

(1) **rope   cat   cup**   (repeat twice)

Make sure the children have enough time to make their choice, then go on to the next question. Say:

(2) **doll   man   door**   (repeat twice)

Continue in the same way with the questions on Page 2. Say:

*Turn over and look at the pictures at the top of the next page. Now there are **three** that start with the same sound, but there is still just one odd one out.* (Repeat each set of words, as above.)

(3) **goat   girl   key   goal**
(4) **hill   bath   hen   hat**
(5) **tap   fish   tick   tart**
(6) **pan   paw   kite   pen**

Look at the next page.

Administration

Literacy Baseline

Phonological awareness: rhymes
(Page 3)

These are to establish the extent to which a child can detect rhyming words. As before, all the words are read aloud by you, with the pictures as memory aids for the children. It is important that you do not separate or unduly emphasise the rhyming part of the word.

The first question is for practice. Say:

*Now I want you to listen to the **ends** of words and tell me which is the odd one out. I'll do the first one with you:*

(P)   ***pan   log   van***   (repeat twice)

*Can you hear the 'an' at the end of **pan** and **van**? So **pan** and **van** are the same, and **log** is the odd one out. Put a line under **log**.*

Check the children understand what they have to do.

Now try these on your own. (Repeat each set of words, as above.)

(7)   ***peg   toe   bow***
(8)   ***hen   pen   men   leg***

Turn over and look at the next page.

Literacy concepts
(Pages 4 and 5)

There are no practice questions in this section. The principle of underlining a choice should by now have been established.

Point to the first box (304, p, not, !).
(9)   *Draw a line under the **word**.*

Point to the next box (5, £, S, ?).
(10)   *Draw a line under the **letter**.*

Point to the next box (Once, not so very long ago,).
(11)   *Draw a line under the **first word** in the box.*

16

Point to the picture and say:
(12) *Look at the picture. I want you to draw a line under the **name of the book**.*

Look at the next page.

Point to the picture.
(13) *Draw a line under the **name of the person who wrote the book**.*

Point to the first box (Once, not so very long ago, there lived a cat called Stan.).
(14) *Draw a line under the **full stop**.*

Point to the next box (Once, not so very long ago, there lived a cat called Stan.).
(15) *Draw a line under a **capital letter**.*

Turn over and look at the next page.

Letters: names
(Page 6)

These questions are to establish whether a child can match a letter with its **name**.

There are no practice questions in this section.

Point to the first box of letters in the top set of boxes (q, s, w, x, y, z).
(16) *Draw a line under the **z**.*

Check only one letter has been underlined.

Point to the next box of letters (b, d, g, p, q, t).
(17) *Draw a line under the **p**.*

Point to the next box of letters (a, c, n, u, v, w).
(18) *Draw a line under the **u**.*

Point to the next box of letters (A, B, D, M, O, P).
(19) *Draw a line under the **D**.*

Letters: sounds
(Page 6)

These questions are to establish whether a child can match a letter with its **sound**. The examples in brackets are for your guidance as to which sound is intended. Examples of words containing the sounds should not be given to the children.

Point to the first box of letters in the second set of boxes (d, f, k, p, s, t).
(20) *Draw a line under the letter that makes this sound: 't'.*

Point to the next box of letters (F, G, K, M, O, Q).
(21) *Draw a line under the letter that makes this sound: 'g'* (as in gate).

Point to the next box of letters (A, G, M, N, T, Z).
(22) *Draw a line under the letter that makes this sound: 'n'.*

Point to the next box of letters (A, E, F, I, M, O).
(23) *Draw a line under the letter that makes this sound: 'e'* (as in egg).

Look at the next page.

Reading: picture to word
(Pages 7 and 8)

The first question is for practice.

(P) *Now you have to choose which one of these words goes with the picture* (point at the words, then the picture). *It's a picture of a dog, so you are looking for the word* **dog**. *When you find it, put a line under it. If you are not sure which word is* **dog***, make a guess.*

Make sure that the children know what they have to do. Give whatever help is necessary with this practice question.

Do not read out the words in subsequent questions. However, if a child asks for help in identifying a **picture**, you may say what it is.

(24) *Now try this one on your own* (picture of **cup**).

(25) *Now do this one* (picture of **tap**).

(26) *Turn over and look at the top picture and words on the next page. You have still got to find the word that goes with the picture and put a line under it* (picture of **television**).

(27, 28) *Now do the next two on your own* (pictures of **book**, **star**).

Look at the next page.

Reading: word to picture
(Pages 9 and 10)

The first question is for practice.

(P) *Now you have to choose which of these pictures goes with this word* (point at the pictures, then the word). *The word is **cat**, so you are looking for a picture of a cat. When you find it, put a line under it.*

Make sure that the children know what they have to do. Give whatever help is necessary with this practice question. **Do not read out the word** in subsequent questions, but, as before, if a child asks for help in identifying a **picture**, you may say what it is.

(29) *Now try this one on your own* (**tree**). *If you are not sure what the word is, put a line under the one you **think** is right.*

(30) Repeat for the next question (**bag**).

(31) *Turn over and look at the top word on the next page. You have still got to find the picture that goes with the word and put a line under it* (**chocolate**).

Now look at the words and pictures at the bottom of the page.

Reading: sentence to picture
(Pages 10 and 11)

There are no practice questions in this section.

Point at the box containing the sentence (**The boy has got a net in his hand.**).

(32) *Now you must read what it says in this box. Choose the picture that goes with it and put a line under it.*

Check that the children understand what they have to do, but do not give any help with working out what the correct answer is.

(33) Repeat the instruction for the remaining question (**The man is reading a book to his son.**).

Spelling
(Pages 11 and 12)

(34) Point to the bottom box and ask children to write their **name** (their first name, given name or name they are most familiar with) on the line. Do not give assistance as this is part of the test.

Ask them then to turn over and to try to write the following words on the lines. If they are not sure of what the right letters are, they should do as well as they can. Allow enough time for all children to complete a word before going on to the next one. Do not give feedback on whether words have been correctly spelled.

(35) *pet* (repeat each word twice)
(36) *lip*
(37) *bun*
(38) *stop*
(39) *time*
(40) *funny*

Administration: RPT1

Group size
The test is designed to allow it to be administered to whole classes or large groups. It may also be used with smaller numbers of children where this is preferred.

Timing
No time limit is set for the test. After initial instructions from you on how the questions are to be answered, the children work through the test at their own pace. They should be allowed as much time as they need to attempt all the questions. Most children will complete the test within one hour – typically 45-50 minutes. However, it is important that slower-working children have ample opportunity to work to the end of the test without time pressure.

It is recommended that the test be completed in a single session, although a short break may be incorporated to avoid fatigue. Where a single session is not possible, children will need to be reminded of how questions should be answered at the start of the second session.

Children who do not finish the test
All children should be encouraged to do their best and to attempt as many questions as they can. In practice, though, there will be cases where children do not work through to the end of the test. In many such cases it may well be reasonable to assume that unattempted questions would not have been correctly answered. In some instances, however, the achieved score will *under*estimate the child's reading comprehension level (meaning that subsequent progress may be *over*estimated). The only general advice that can be given is that the results of children who do not complete the test must be interpreted with caution.

Preparation
Each child should have a copy of the test booklet and writing materials.

You will need a copy of the test booklet as well as these instructions.

Test conditions
It is important that the children work on their own, without copying, discussion or collaboration. However, you may give any additional explanation necessary to help children understand the way they should answer the questions.

The test is not a test of memory. It is important that, where there are questions about a reading text, children do not under-perform because they have tried to answer questions from memory of the text. *Repeat the advice to answer by referring back to the text as often as the children need it.*

Method of answering

Most answers are made by underlining a choice. If necessary, however, children can indicate their answers by pointing, with you or another adult underlining on their behalf. If the children you are working with are more used to indicating their answers by some other means (such as by putting a ring round their chosen answer) rather than by underlining, they may answer in this way. The instructions you give the children will need to be changed accordingly.

Only one choice should be selected in each question. Answers may be altered by rubbing or crossing out.

In order to allow children to work at their own pace, the way that each question type is answered is explained to them at the start of the test. As the test progresses, you will need to check that children have remembered what they have to do, and give further reminders and guidance as necessary.

Giving RPT1

- Give each child a copy of the test booklet with his or her name entered in the box at the top. Ask them to write their first name on the label on the front cover.

- Introduce the booklet by explaining that:

  - first they are going to answer some questions in the booklet;

  - then they are going to read some stories and a poem about food and answer questions about them;

  - you are going to explain how they are going to answer the different sorts of questions before they start.

- Go through the whole booklet with the children *before they start work on it*, as follows.

  - Ask the children to open their booklet and look at page 2. Explain that they have to answer the questions by choosing the right word to go with the picture and putting a line under it. They should only put a line under *one* of the words. Draw their attention to the practice question. Ask them to read the four words with you and then put a line under the word *tin*. Check that they have all completed this in the right way. If any have not, explain the procedure to them again.

  - Ask the children to look at page 3 and read the instruction at the top of the page with them. Again, check that they all understand what they have to do.

  - Ask the children to turn to page 4 of the booklet and explain that they will have to read this story and then answer questions 7 – 9 in the top box on page 5 by putting a line under the right picture.

- ❏ Ask them to look at the questions in the bottom box and read the instruction with them. Explain that the story does not tell us what Mum, Dad, Gran and Joe actually say to each other, but in questions 10 – 12 they have to think who *might* have said each of the sentences and put a line under the right picture. Do not work through the practice item at this point, as children will not have read the story: the practice item should be used, either with individuals or groups, once they have read the story. (You may wish to ask them to indicate to you when they have reached this point in the test.)

- ❏ Ask the children to turn to page 6 of the booklet and explain that they have to read this story and then answer the questions about it on pages 7 and 8 by putting a line under the right answer. (Remind them that they can look back from page 8 to the story on page 6.)

- ❏ Ask the children to look at page 9 of the booklet and explain that they have to read the poem in the top box and then answer the questions about it in the bottom box by putting a line under the right answer.

- ❏ Ask the children to turn to page 10 of the booklet and explain that they have to read the story and, when they come to a box containing three words, they have to put a line under the word that fits the meaning of the story. Suggest that they read through the whole page once before they choose the right word from each box.

- ❏ Explain that the story continues on page 11, but there are some words missing. Each time they come to a space, they have to decide what the missing word is and write it in. Emphasise that they should write only one word in each space. Help may be given with spelling, but incorrect spelling is not penalised.

- ❏ Explain that if they do not remember how to answer a question while they are doing the test, they should ask you and you will help them.

■ The children can then work through the questions at their own pace.

■ During the test:

- ❏ Remind the children that they should refer back to the stories to help them answer the questions and that they should ask you if they do not remember how to answer any of the questions. Remind them they should only underline *one* of the choices in each question.

- ❏ Check periodically on the children's progress, particularly those who you think may have difficulty. Encourage them to keep going and to answer as many questions as they can.

- ❏ As children finish reading the story on page 4, work through the practice question on page 5 with them, either individually or in groups. If they have not already completed questions 7, 8 and 9, remind them to go back to them.

■ When the children have completed the test, collect in the booklets for marking.

Administration: RPT2

Group size
The test is designed to allow it to be administered to whole classes or large groups. It may also be used with smaller numbers of children where this is preferred.

Timing
No time limit is set for the test. After initial instructions from you on how the questions are to be answered, the children work through the test at their own pace. They should be allowed as much time as they need to attempt all the questions. Most children will complete the test within one hour – typically 45-50 minutes. However, it is important that slower-working children have ample opportunity to work to the end of the test without time pressure.

It is recommended that the test be completed in a single session, although a short break may be incorporated to avoid fatigue. Where a single session is not possible, children will need to be reminded of how questions should be answered at the start of the second session.

Children who do not finish the test
All children should be encouraged to do their best and to attempt as many questions as they can. In practice, though, there will be cases where children do not work through to the end of the test. In many such cases it may well be reasonable to assume that unattempted questions would not have been correctly answered. In some instances, however, the achieved score will *under*estimate the child's reading comprehension level (meaning that subsequent progress may be *over*estimated). The only general advice that can be given is that the results of children who do not complete the test must be interpreted with caution.

Preparation
Each child should have a copy of the test booklet and writing materials.

You will need a copy of the test booklet as well as these instructions.

Test conditions
It is important that the children work on their own, without copying, discussion or collaboration. However, you may give any additional explanation necessary to help children understand the way they should answer the questions.

The test is not a test of memory. It is important that, where there are questions about a reading text, children do not under-perform because they have tried to answer questions from memory of the text. *Repeat the advice to answer by referring back to the text as often as the children need it.*

Method of answering

Most answers are made by underlining a choice. If necessary, however, children can indicate their answers by pointing, with you or another adult underlining on their behalf. If the children you are working with are more used to indicating their answers by some other means (such as by putting a ring round their chosen answer) rather than by underlining, they may answer in this way. The instructions you give the children will need to be changed accordingly.

Only one choice should be selected in each question. Answers may be altered by rubbing or crossing out.

In order to allow children to work at their own pace, the way that each question type is answered is explained to them at the start of the test. As the test progresses, you will need to check that children have remembered what they have to do, and give further reminders and guidance as necessary.

Giving RPT2

- Give each child a copy of the test booklet with his or her name on.

- Introduce the booklet by explaining that:

    - first they are going to answer some questions in the booklet;

    - then they are going to read some stories and an information passage about fish and answer questions about them;

    - you are going to explain how they are going to answer the different sorts of questions before they start.

- Go through the whole booklet with the children *before they start work on it*, as follows.

    - Ask the children to look at the front cover of their booklet. Explain that they have to answer the questions by choosing the right word to go with the picture and putting a line under it. They should only put a line under *one* of the words. Draw their attention to the practice question. Ask them to read the four words with you and put a line under the word *net*. Check that they have all completed this in the right way. If any have not, explain the procedure to them again.

    - Ask the children to look at page 2 and explain that they are going to read this story and then answer questions 4 and 5 on page 3 by putting a line under the right picture.

    - Ask them to look at the bottom box on page 3. Read through the instruction with them, and make sure they understand what they have to do.

- Ask them to look at questions 10 to 13 on page 5. Explain that they should read the story on page 4, and then answer these questions.

- Ask them to look at questions 14 and 15 at the bottom of page 5. Explain that although neither Dad, Mum nor Uncle Steve actually say these things in the story on page 4, they have to decide which of them *might* have said each of the sentences. Check that they all understand what they have to do.

- Ask them to look at the questions on page 7. Explain that these questions are about the story on page 6. Again, the questions should be answered by underlining the right answer.

- Ask the children to turn to page 9 and explain that they have to answer these questions about the *Electric Eels* passage on page 8 by putting a tick in the correct box.

- Ask the children to turn to page 10 of the booklet and explain that they have to read the passage about *Flat-fish* and when they come to a box containing four words, they have to put a line under the word that fits the meaning of the passage. Suggest that they read through the whole page once before they choose the right word from each box. Check that they all understand what they have to do.

- Explain that the passage continues on page 11, but there are some words missing. Each time they come to a space, they have to decide what the missing word is and write it in. Emphasise that they should write only one word in each space. Help may be given with spelling, but incorrect spelling is not penalised.

- Explain that if they do not remember how to answer a question while they are doing the test, they should ask you and you will help them.

■ During the test:

- Remind the children that they should refer back to the stories to help them answer the questions and that they should ask you if they do not remember how to answer any of the questions. Remind them they should only underline *one* of the choices in each question.

- Check periodically on the children's progress, particularly those who you think may have difficulty. Encourage them to keep going and to answer as many questions as they can.

■ When the children have completed the test, collect in the booklets for marking.

Marking: Literacy Baseline

Ignore the practice questions when you are marking the tests. Award one mark for each correct answer. No marks should be awarded for multiple choice questions where more than one choice has been selected. Do not award half marks.

Phonological awareness: initial sounds

(practice)
1. rope
2. man
3. key
4. bath
5. fish
6. kite

Phonological awareness: rhymes

(practice)
7. peg
8. leg

Literacy concepts

9. not
10. S
11. Once
12. title
13. author
14. full stop
15. capital letter

Letters: names

16. z
17. p
18. u
19. D

Letters: sounds

20. t
21. G
22. N
23. E

Reading: picture to word

(practice)
24. cup
25. tap
26. television
27. book
28. star

Reading: word to picture

(practice)
29. tree
30. bag
31. chocolate

Reading: sentence to picture

32. Picture 1 (top left)
33. Picture 2 (top right)

Spelling

34. child's name
35. pet
36. lip
37. bun
38. stop
39. time
40. funny

Marking: RPT1

Ignore the practice questions when you are marking the tests. Award one mark for each correct answer. No marks should be awarded for multiple choice questions where more than one choice has been selected. Do not award half marks.

Picture/word

(practice)
1. banana
2. sweet
3. spoon

Word identification

4. cheese
5. tart
6. honey

The Lost Cakes

7. Dad
8. Joe
9. Mum
(practice)
10. Joe
11. Mum
12. Mum

The Pudding

13. Gran
14. Jemma
15. doesn't say
16. Tiger
17. Jemma
18. Jemma
19. Tiger
20. Gran
21. because Jemma added extra ingredients

Karen doesn't like a cone

22. "I don't like them without ice cream."
23. She lets her ice cream melt.

The Bus Cake

24. cakes
25. looks
26. runaway
27. man
28. went/drove/sped
29. and
30. never
31. cake/one
32. like

Marking: RPT2

Ignore the practice questions when you are marking the tests. Award one mark for each correct answer. No marks should be awarded for multiple choice questions where more than one choice has been selected. Do not award half marks.

Picture/word

(practice)
1. starfish
2. anchor
3. diver

Never Trust a Talking Fish

4. Picture 3 (fish with jewel)
5. Picture 2 (fish with nothing in mouth)

Word identification

6. whale
7. mermaid
8. oyster
9. salmon

Uncle Steve and the Goldfish

10. Dad
11. No one
12. Uncle Steve
13. Mum
14. Uncle Steve
15. Dad

The Grass Sharks

16. because it was part of the trick
17. She thought it was funny that the children believed in the grass sharks.
18. The teachers had been joking.
19. Tina
20. Sam

Electric Eels

21. false
22. true
23. true
24. false
25. true
26. doesn't say
27. doesn't say

Flat-fish

28. not
29. Young
30. changes
31. side
32. good
33. difficult/hard
34. bigger/larger
35. eat/kill

Whole booklet

36. Never trust a talking fish
37. Flat-fish
38. The grass sharks

Using and interpreting the conversion tables

Introduction

The tables on the pages 36-41 allow you to convert each child's 'raw score' (i.e. the number of questions correctly answered) into the following forms:

- standardised scores;
- reading ages;
- ability scale scores.

The tables on pages 42-44 are used to derive *progress* 'quotients' and percentile equivalents based on the difference between scores on the Literacy Baseline and RPT1 (page 42), the Literacy Baseline and RPT2 (page 43) and RPT1 and RPT2 (page 44).

Standardised scores

A *standardised score* can be obtained by following these steps:

1. read down the raw score column at the left or right sides of the table to the row which gives the reader's raw score;

2. read along the row until the column which corresponds with the reader's chronological age in years and completed months is reached;

3. the number at this intersection is the standardised score for a child of that age and raw score level.

Standardised scores are on a normative scale with a mean of 100, i.e. the closer a score is to 100, the closer the reader is to the average or norm for their age group. Approximately 34 per cent of children in a group *typical* of their age will earn standardised scores between 100 and 115 and a further 34 per cent would score in the 85 to 100 range. (This does not mean that you should necessarily expect the same pattern of scores in your own school or class, however.) So, for example, a standardised score of 94 would be somewhat below average, but not greatly so. A standardised score of 120, on the other hand, would place a child in the top 10 per cent for their age in terms of reading comprehension. Percentile equivalents are:

Standardised score:	70	75	80	85	90	95	100	105	110	115	120	125	130
Percentile:	2	5	9	16	26	37	50	63	74	84	91	95	98

The standardised score tables for the Literacy Baseline and for RPT1 and RPT2 incorporate an adjustment for differences in test performance which are attributable to differences in chronological age. Thus a child who earns a standardised score of 100 can be considered average only in relation to other children of the same age in years and completed months. The same raw score would be *above* average for younger children and *below* average if they were older.

This adjustment for maturity can be helpful in considering the progress of beginning readers. For example, the very youngest children in a class might otherwise be too readily judged to be performing less well than 'expected'. However, it should be noted that the importance of chronological age differences diminishes with age. For example, the correlation between score and chronological age only just reached statistical significance in the year groups of children who took RPT2.

Using confidence limits to interpret standardised scores

A child's standardised score on a test should be regarded as an estimate of his or her ability and may well be subject to a margin of error. The *reliability coefficient* for an educational test is used to find the *standard error of measurement*, which is the usual way in which this margin of error is expressed statistically. The more reliable the test, the smaller the standard error of measurement will be and thus the narrower will be the margin of error associated with the test.

The standard error of measurement is used to establish, at a chosen level of probability, the range in which a child's 'true' score lies. For this series a 90 per cent level of confidence has been adopted. This means that for the great majority of children – those obtaining standardised scores in the range 80 - 120 – we can be 90 per cent certain that their 'true' score lies within ±8 points of their obtained score on the Literacy Baseline, and ±7 points on RPT1 and RPT2. For children scoring further from the average of 100 – with standardised scores below 80 or above 120 – the confidence limits are ±10 points of standardised score on the Literacy Baseline and ±9 points on RPT1 and RPT2. Note that for such low and high scores error is more likely to be in the direction of the mean: for a child achieving a low score on the test, there is a greater probability that his or her true ability has been underestimated rather than overestimated; conversely, a high score is more likely to be an overestimate than an underestimate of a child's ability.

Reading ages

The *reading age* tables for each test make it possible to find a reading age for raw scores greater than zero and less than full marks. To do this, locate the raw score in the left hand column, and read across to the second column to find the reading age in months, or to the third column to find the reading age in years and months.

The tables are based on the linear relationship between age and ability found in the year group samples of children who took the tests. However, the tables have been extrapolated to give estimated reading ages across the full range of scores. This means that some reading age values lie outside the actual chronological age range of the children who provided the data on which the tables are based. Shading is used to indicate the actual chronological age range of the children in each sample.

The reading age scale has long been popular in UK primary schools as a way of expressing children's reading attainment. However, it has been noted that chronological age is only a rough guide to how well a child can be expected to read. While there is a general underlying trend for reading to develop with chronological age, the statistical relationship is modest rather than strong, diminishing with age.

As a consequence of this weakness of the association between age and reading ability, the reading age a child earns will depend upon the particular method used to scale the test. A variety of more or less equally acceptable ways is employed across different published reading tests to derive age scores from raw scores and it is quite possible that this would lead to quite different results for the same child across a battery of reading tests. Other factors such as difference in the time of year at which tests were standardised add to the problem of comparability. Reading ages in general, therefore, should be interpreted with considerable caution.

Ability scale scores

The tables for reading ages also contain a column giving *ability scale scores*. To find the appropriate ability scale score, locate the raw score in the left-hand column, and read across to the fourth column.

This scale expresses a reader's attainment relative to the trait or dimension measured by the test, i.e. reading comprehension. A scaled score of 100 represents the mid-point of the ability range measured by a test scaled in this way. Differences in scores are considered to be directly comparable independent of where they occur on the scale. For example, the difference in ability between a reader who scores 90 and one who scores 100 can be considered the same as the difference between a score of 110 and a score of 120. Standardised score differences cannot be interpreted in this way. Scale scores are useful for evaluating the range of ability differences in a class and for grouping/matching children for teaching purposes according to their ability.

Progress scores

The tables on pages 42 to 44 give progress norms for children who take a successive pair of tests:

- Literacy Baseline followed by RPT1;
- Literacy Baseline followed by RPT2;
- RPT1 followed by RPT2.

Progress is expressed in the following forms:

- a progress quotient (a standardised score for progress);
- percentile equivalents.

To obtain a progress score, proceed as follows:

1. subtract the child's reading age for the first test taken from the reading age for the second test to give the number of months of progress made;

2. locate the column representing the number of completed months between the two tests;

3. find the row which corresponds with the number of months of progress made (as found in step 1, above) in that column;

4. read across to find the progress quotient.

Interpreting progress quotients

The *progress quotients* are standardised scores, but no adjustment for age is incorporated. The term 'quotient' has been adopted to avoid confusion with the standardised scores for attainment which are tabulated on pages 36 to 41. No adjustment is made for chronological age, because the results of the standardisation of the test showed this to be unnecessary. For example, younger children did not on average make less (or more) progress than older children.

As with standardised attainment scores, the progress quotients are scaled with a mean of 100 and a standard deviation of 15. Thus a quotient of 100 means a child is making average progress, and the majority of children will earn quotients within 15 points either side of 100.

The progress scores are also expressed in terms of the nearest *percentile*. Percentiles indicate the percentage of cases who would be expected to score below a specified point, i.e. make less progress. A reader making 12 months' progress over a period of nine completed months between taking the Literacy Baseline and RPT1 is placed above the 63rd percentile for progress: 63 per cent of children are estimated to make less than 12 months' progress in a nine month period.

The tables include progress scores with zero or minus values. Some children in the standardisation sample appeared to 'deteriorate' in performance. However, the percentage was much smaller than that making at least some positive progress. It is also important to note that there is considerable variation in the amount of progress in months which might be considered 'average'. For instance, on being tested on RPT1 nine months after taking the Literacy Baseline, 'average' children (i.e. the 50 per cent of children between the 25th and 75th percentile) may make anything from one to fifteen months' worth of progress. It is only progress outside this range that should be considered exceptional.

In the tables for RPT1 to RPT2 and Literacy Baseline to RPT2, progress quotients have not been provided below 80, i.e. for approximately the ten per cent of children making the least progress. Within this group there was very great variation, with a small number of children deteriorating in reading age in the range of two to three years. Given the relatively small number of children involved and the considerable variation in their (negative) progress scores, it was not possible to extend the conversion tables to cover this group.

Using and interpreting the conversion tables

Case study: Louisa

Louisa answered correctly 20 questions when she took the Literacy Baseline test in mid October. Her birthday was on July 3rd and her age at the time was 5 years and 3 (completed) months.

To obtain her standardised score her teacher first found the 5:3 column which corresponded with Louisa's age in the table on page 36. The teacher then read down the column until reaching the row which corresponded with Louisa's raw score of 20. The figure 105 appears at this intersection. This was Louisa's standardised score and meant she could be considered average, if not slightly above average, for her age. Using the table on page 37, the teacher read down the raw score column to the row which corresponded with 20. This gave Louisa a reading age of 5 years 5 months (65 months) which was two months in advance of her chronological age. Reading across to the right-hand column, the teacher found a raw score of 20 corresponded to an ability scale score of 98. This put Louisa slightly below, but close to, the mid-point (100) on the trait measured by the Literacy Baseline test. Overall Louisa appeared to be very much average for her age.

Nine months later, just before the end of the summer term in the same school year, the class was given RPT1. Louisa answered correctly 13 questions on the test. At the time of testing her age in years and completed months was 6:0. The teacher located this column on page 38 and read down to the raw score row for 13 to find Louisa's standardised score was 109. This placed Louisa in the 'higher average' group for her chronological age. In the table for reading ages on page 39, a raw score of 13 corresponds with a reading age of 6 years and 7 months (79 months). This was 7 months above Louisa's chronological age. Her ability scale score of 102 puts her performance above the mid-point of the continuum measured by the test.

Subtracting Louisa's Literacy Baseline age from her reading age on RPT1 gave a difference of 14 months. Clearly, 14 months' progress in just 9 months looked promising, but the table on page 42 allowed the teacher to interpret this more precisely.

As there were nine completed months between the two test sessions, the teacher used the '9 months' column in the table on page 42 to evaluate the progress Louisa had made. The teacher read down the column to locate the row for 14 months' progress in the body of the table. This row lies within the mid-band for average performance in the table. Reading across the row, the teacher found that Louisa's progress 'quotient' was 107.

To understand more precisely what this meant, the teacher inspected the right-hand column of the table. She noted that Louisa was at the 68th percentile equivalent, i.e. she had 'out-progressed' over 68 per cent of the children involved in the original standardisation of the test.

During the year Louisa had emerged as a careful if not cautious worker who was sometimes unwilling to commit herself to an answer if she was unsure. The teacher noted that this was reflected in the way she had completed RPT1: Louisa had not attempted three questions in the first half of the test. The teacher suspected that, if Louisa had been willing to make a 'best guess', she would probably have selected the correct answer. This meant that, if anything, the obtained results were a conservative estimate of Louisa's progress over the year.

Case study: Year 1 class

Mrs K. was aware that some of the parents of children in her year 1 class were very 'reading age conscious' and that there were also some anxieties about the effectiveness of the way reading was being taught in the school. In view of these concerns Mrs K. felt it was important to keep her class's progress under review. On November 20th she gave all the children the Literacy Baseline test. They achieved a mean raw score of 15.8. The mean age of the class at the time of testing was 5 years and 5 months and this meant the average standardised score for the class was 95 and their average reading age was 5 years. To some extent the result was depressed by the presence of a group of children who scored less than 15 – the suggested cut-score for identifying children who are at risk of performing poorly when re-tested for reading comprehension on RPT1. None of the children managed a reading age that was more than four months above their chronological age.

Follow-up testing with RPT1 took place on 21st May. This was the earliest date at which re-testing could take place if the progress scores table on page 42 were to be used – Mrs K. was keen to obtain information about the children's progress as soon as possible. The average reading age difference between the Literacy Baseline test and RPT1 was 4.9 months, somewhat less than an 'expected' average of 6 months. However, most children showed signs of positive progress, some had managed to gain more than 6 months and Mrs K. was re-assured to find that only one child had deteriorated and only a few had made zero progress. Half of the children with raw scores of less than 15 on the Literacy Baseline test had managed to make positive progress, although most of the 'zero progress' children were also found in this group.

It was evident to Mrs K. that, while there were individual success stories, there was a genuine possibility that a class which had in general started from a comparatively low 'baseline' position could be in danger of gradually slipping further behind. The decision to follow-up test after only six months had provided a useful early warning of this possibility and an opportunity to consider ways of redressing the position.

Literacy Baseline conversion tables

raw score	chronological age in years and completed months												raw score
	5:0	5:1	5:2	5:3	5:4	5:5	5:6	5:7	5:8	5:9	5:10	5:11	
1	70-	70-	70-	70-	70-	70-	70-	70-	70-	70-	70-	70-	1
2	72	71	70-	70-	70-	70-	70-	70-	70-	70-	70-	70-	2
3	74	72	71	70	70-	70-	70-	70-	70-	70-	70-	70-	3
4	76	74	73	72	71	70	70-	70-	70-	70-	70-	70-	4
5	79	77	75	74	73	72	71	70	70-	70-	70-	70-	5
6	82	80	78	77	75	74	73	72	71	70-	70-	70-	6
7	86	83	81	80	78	76	75	74	73	72	71	70-	7
8	89	86	84	82	81	79	78	76	75	74	73	72	8
9	91	89	87	85	83	82	80	79	78	77	76	75	9
10	94	91	89	87	86	84	83	81	80	79	78	77	10
11	96	94	92	90	88	86	85	83	82	81	80	78	11
12	98	96	94	92	90	88	87	85	84	83	82	80	12
13	99	98	96	94	92	90	89	87	86	85	83	82	13
14	101	99	97	96	94	92	90	89	88	86	85	84	14
15	102	101	99	97	95	94	92	91	89	88	87	86	15
16	103	102	101	99	97	95	94	92	91	89	88	87	16
17	105	103	102	101	99	97	95	94	92	91	90	89	17
18	106	105	103	102	101	99	97	95	94	92	91	90	18
19	108	106	105	103	102	100	99	97	95	94	92	91	19
20	109	107	106	105	103	102	100	98	97	95	94	92	20
21	110	109	107	106	105	103	102	100	98	96	95	94	21
22	112	110	109	107	106	104	103	101	100	98	96	95	22
23	114	112	110	109	107	106	104	103	101	99	98	96	23
24	115	114	112	110	109	107	106	104	103	101	99	97	24
25	117	116	114	112	111	109	107	106	104	102	100	99	25
26	118	117	116	114	113	111	109	107	106	104	102	100	26
27	120	118	117	116	115	113	111	109	107	106	104	102	27
28	122	120	119	118	116	115	113	111	109	107	106	104	28
29	124	122	120	119	118	117	115	113	111	109	107	106	29
30	126	124	123	121	119	118	117	115	113	111	109	107	30
31	128	127	125	123	122	120	118	117	115	113	111	109	31
32	130	129	127	126	124	122	120	119	117	115	113	111	32
33	133	131	130	128	127	125	123	121	119	117	115	113	33
34	136	134	133	131	129	128	126	124	122	119	118	116	34
35	140+	139	136	134	132	131	129	127	125	122	120	118	35
36	140+	140+	140+	139	136	134	132	130	128	126	123	121	36
37	140+	140+	140+	140+	140+	139	136	134	132	129	127	124	37
38	140+	140+	140+	140+	140+	140+	140+	140	136	134	131	128	38
39	140+	140+	140+	140+	140+	140+	140+	140+	140+	140+	137	133	39
40	140+	140+	140+	140+	140+	140+	140+	140+	140+	140+	140+	140+	40
	5:0	5:1	5:2	5:3	5:4	5:5	5:6	5:7	5:8	5:9	5:10	5:11	

raw score	6:0	6:1	6:2	6:3	6:4	raw score
1	70-	70-	70-	70-	70-	1
2	70-	70-	70-	70-	70-	2
3	70-	70-	70-	70-	70-	3
4	70-	70-	70-	70-	70-	4
5	70-	70-	70-	70-	70-	5
6	70-	70-	70-	70-	70-	6
7	70-	70-	70-	70-	70-	7
8	70	70-	70-	70-	70-	8
9	73	72	70	70-	70-	9
10	76	74	73	72	70	10
11	77	76	75	74	73	11
12	79	78	77	76	75	12
13	81	80	79	78	77	13
14	83	82	81	80	79	14
15	85	83	82	81	80	15
16	86	85	84	83	82	16
17	87	86	85	84	83	17
18	89	88	87	86	85	18
19	90	89	88	87	86	19
20	91	90	89	88	87	20
21	92	91	90	89	88	21
22	94	93	91	90	89	22
23	95	94	93	91	90	23
24	96	95	94	93	92	24
25	97	96	95	94	93	25
26	99	97	96	95	94	26
27	100	98	97	96	95	27
28	102	100	98	97	96	28
29	104	101	100	98	97	29
30	105	103	101	99	98	30
31	107	105	103	101	99	31
32	109	107	105	103	101	32
33	112	109	107	105	103	33
34	114	112	109	107	105	34
35	116	114	112	109	107	35
36	118	116	114	112	109	36
37	122	119	117	115	112	37
38	126	123	120	117	115	38
39	130	127	124	120	118	39
40	137	133	129	125	122	40
	6:0	6:1	6:2	6:3	6:4	

raw score	reading age		ability scale score
	months	years & months	
1			73
2			77
3			80
4			82
5	48	4 : 0	84
6	49	4 : 1	85
7	50	4 : 2	85
8	52	4 : 4	87
9	53	4 : 5	88
10	54	4 : 6	89
11	55	4 : 7	90
12	57	4 : 9	91
13	58	4 :10	92
14	59	4 :11	93
15	60	5 : 0	94
16	60	5 : 0	94
17	61	5 : 1	95
18	62	5 : 2	96
19	64	5 : 4	97
20	65	5 : 5	98
21	65	5 : 5	98
22	66	5 : 6	99
23	67	5 : 7	100
24	68	5 : 8	101
25	69	5 : 9	102
26	71	5 :11	103
27	72	6 : 0	104
28	72	6 : 0	104
29	74	6 : 2	106
30	75	6 : 3	107
31	76	6 : 4	108
32	77	6 : 5	109
33	80	6 : 8	111
34	81	6 : 9	112
35	83	6 :11	114
36	86	7 : 2	116
37	89	7 : 5	119
38	94	7 :10	123
39	101	8 : 5	129

RPT1 conversion tables

raw score	\multicolumn{12}{c}{chronological age in years and completed months}	raw score
	5:8	5:9	5:10	5:11	6:0	6:1	6:2	6:3	6:4	6:5	6:6	6:7	
1	93	91	88	85	83	81	80	78	78	77	76	75	1
2	96	95	93	91	89	87	85	84	83	82	81	80	2
3	98	97	96	94	92	91	89	88	86	86	85	84	3
4	101	99	98	96	95	93	92	91	90	88	87	87	4
5	102	101	100	98	97	96	94	93	92	91	90	89	5
6	104	103	101	100	99	97	96	95	94	93	92	91	6
7	106	104	103	102	100	99	98	97	96	95	94	93	7
8	107	106	105	103	102	101	100	98	97	96	95	94	8
9	108	107	106	105	104	102	101	100	99	98	97	96	9
10	110	108	107	106	105	104	103	101	100	99	98	97	10
11	111	110	109	108	107	105	104	103	102	101	99	98	11
12	112	111	110	109	108	107	106	104	103	102	101	100	12
13	114	112	111	110	109	108	107	106	104	103	102	101	13
14	115	114	113	112	110	109	108	107	106	105	103	102	14
15	116	115	114	113	112	110	109	108	107	106	105	104	15
16	117	116	115	114	113	112	111	109	108	107	106	105	16
17	118	117	116	116	115	113	112	111	109	108	107	106	17
18	118	118	117	117	116	115	114	112	111	110	108	107	18
19	119	119	118	118	117	116	115	114	112	111	110	109	19
20	120	120	119	119	118	117	116	115	114	113	111	110	20
21	122	121	120	120	119	118	118	117	116	114	113	111	21
22	123	123	122	121	120	120	119	118	117	116	114	113	22
23	125	124	123	122	122	121	120	119	118	117	116	115	23
24	126	125	125	124	123	122	122	121	120	119	118	116	24
25	128	127	126	126	125	124	123	122	121	120	119	118	25
26	130	129	128	128	127	126	125	124	123	122	121	120	26
27	132	131	130	130	129	128	127	126	125	124	123	122	27
28	134	134	133	132	131	130	129	129	128	127	126	125	28
29	139	138	136	135	134	133	132	131	130	129	128	127	29
30	140+	140+	140+	140+	139	137	136	135	134	133	132	130	30
31	140+	140+	140+	140+	140+	140+	140+	140+	139	138	136	134	31
32	140+	140+	140+	140+	140+	140+	140+	140+	140+	140+	140+	140+	32
	5:8	5:9	5:10	5:11	6:0	6:1	6:2	6:3	6:4	6:5	6:6	6:7	

raw score	6:8	6:9	6:10	6:11	7:0	7:1	7:2	raw score
1	75	74	73	73	72	71	71	1
2	80	79	78	78	77	76	76	2
3	83	82	82	81	80	80	79	3
4	86	85	84	84	83	82	82	4
5	88	87	86	86	85	85	84	5
6	90	89	88	88	87	86	86	6
7	92	91	90	89	89	88	87	7
8	93	93	92	91	90	89	89	8
9	95	94	93	92	92	91	90	9
10	96	96	95	94	93	92	92	10
11	97	97	96	95	94	94	93	11
12	99	98	97	96	96	95	94	12
13	100	99	98	98	97	96	95	13
14	101	100	99	99	98	97	96	14
15	102	101	101	100	99	98	97	15
16	104	103	102	101	100	99	98	16
17	105	104	103	102	101	100	99	17
18	106	105	104	103	102	101	101	18
19	107	106	105	104	103	102	102	19
20	109	108	106	105	104	104	103	20
21	110	109	108	107	106	105	104	21
22	112	110	109	108	107	106	105	22
23	113	112	110	109	108	107	106	23
24	115	114	112	110	109	108	107	24
25	117	115	114	112	111	109	108	25
26	119	118	116	114	113	111	109	26
27	121	120	118	117	115	113	111	27
28	123	122	121	119	118	115	113	28
29	126	125	123	122	121	119	116	29
30	129	128	127	125	124	122	120	30
31	133	132	130	129	127	125	124	31
32	140+	138	136	134	132	130	128	32
	6:8	6:9	6:10	6:11	7:0	7:1	7:2	

raw score	reading age		ability scale score
	months	years & months	
1	50	4 : 2	84
2	56	4 : 8	88
3	60	5 : 0	90
4	63	5 : 3	92
5	68	5 : 8	95
6	70	5 :10	96
7	71	5 :11	97
8	72	6 : 0	98
9	73	6 : 1	98
10	74	6 : 2	99
11	76	6 : 4	100
12	78	6 : 6	101
13	79	6 : 7	102
14	81	6 : 9	103
15	82	6 :10	104
16	83	6 :11	104
17	84	7 : 0	105
18	86	7 : 2	106
19	87	7 : 3	107
20	88	7 : 4	107
21	89	7 : 5	108
22	91	7 : 7	109
23	93	7 : 9	110
24	94	7 :10	111
25	96	8 : 0	112
26	98	8 : 2	113
27	99	8 : 3	114
28	100	8 : 4	115
29	104	8 : 8	117
30	108	9 : 0	119
31	114	9 : 6	123

RPT2 conversion tables

raw score	\multicolumn{12}{c}{chronological age in years and completed months}	raw score
	6:8	6:9	6:10	6:11	7:0	7:1	7:2	7:3	7:4	7:5	7:6	7:7	
1	74	73	72	72	71	71	71	70	70	70	70	70	1
2	81	81	80	78	77	77	76	76	75	75	75	74	2
3	84	83	83	82	81	81	80	80	79	79	78	78	3
4	87	86	85	85	84	83	83	82	82	81	81	81	4
5	90	88	88	87	86	86	85	85	84	83	83	82	5
6	92	91	90	89	88	87	87	86	86	85	85	84	6
7	94	93	92	91	90	89	88	88	87	87	86	86	7
8	96	94	93	92	91	91	90	89	89	88	88	87	8
9	97	96	95	94	93	92	91	91	90	90	89	89	9
10	99	98	97	96	95	94	93	92	92	91	91	90	10
11	100	99	98	97	96	95	95	94	93	92	92	91	11
12	102	101	100	99	98	97	96	95	94	94	93	92	12
13	103	102	101	100	99	98	97	96	96	95	94	93	13
14	105	104	103	102	101	100	99	98	97	96	95	94	14
15	106	105	104	103	102	101	100	99	98	97	96	96	15
16	107	106	105	104	103	102	101	100	99	98	98	97	16
17	109	108	107	106	105	104	103	102	101	100	99	98	17
18	110	109	108	107	106	105	104	103	102	101	100	99	18
19	111	110	109	108	107	106	105	104	103	102	101	100	19
20	112	112	111	110	109	108	107	106	105	104	103	102	20
21	114	113	112	111	110	109	108	107	106	105	104	103	21
22	115	114	113	113	112	110	109	108	107	106	105	104	22
23	116	116	115	114	113	112	111	110	109	108	107	106	23
24	118	117	116	116	115	114	113	111	110	109	108	107	24
25	119	119	118	117	116	115	114	113	112	111	110	109	25
26	121	120	119	119	118	117	116	115	114	113	111	110	26
27	122	121	121	120	119	119	118	117	116	114	113	112	27
28	124	123	122	122	121	120	119	119	117	116	115	114	28
29	125	124	124	123	123	122	121	120	119	118	117	116	29
30	128	127	126	125	124	124	123	122	121	120	119	118	30
31	130	130	129	128	127	126	125	124	124	123	122	121	31
32	133	132	132	131	130	129	128	127	126	125	124	123	32
33	136	135	134	134	133	132	132	131	130	129	128	126	33
34	140+	140+	139	138	137	136	135	134	134	133	132	131	34
35	140+	140+	140+	140+	140+	140+	140+	140+	139	138	137	135	35
36	140+	140+	140+	140+	140+	140+	140+	140+	140+	140+	140+	140+	36
37	140+	140+	140+	140+	140+	140+	140+	140+	140+	140+	140+	140+	37
38	140+	140+	140+	140+	140+	140+	140+	140+	140+	140+	140+	140+	38
	6:8	6:9	6:10	6:11	7:0	7:1	7:2	7:3	7:4	7:5	7:6	7:7	

raw score	7:8	7:9	7:10	7:11	8:0	8:1	raw score
1	70-	70-	70-	70-	70-	70-	1
2	74	74	73	73	73	72	2
3	77	77	76	76	76	76	3
4	80	79	79	78	78	78	4
5	82	81	81	81	80	80	5
6	84	83	83	82	82	82	6
7	85	85	84	84	84	83	7
8	87	86	86	86	85	85	8
9	88	88	87	87	86	86	9
10	90	89	88	88	87	87	10
11	91	90	90	89	89	88	11
12	92	91	91	90	90	89	12
13	93	92	92	91	91	90	13
14	94	93	93	92	92	91	14
15	95	94	94	93	93	92	15
16	96	95	95	94	94	93	16
17	97	96	96	95	95	94	17
18	98	98	97	96	96	95	18
19	99	99	98	97	97	96	19
20	101	100	99	98	98	97	20
21	102	101	100	99	99	98	21
22	103	102	101	100	100	99	22
23	105	104	103	102	101	100	23
24	106	105	104	103	102	101	24
25	108	106	105	104	103	103	25
26	109	108	107	106	105	104	26
27	111	109	108	107	106	105	27
28	113	111	110	109	108	107	28
29	115	113	112	110	109	108	29
30	117	116	114	113	111	110	30
31	120	118	117	115	114	112	31
32	122	121	120	118	117	115	32
33	125	124	123	121	120	118	33
34	130	128	126	125	123	122	34
35	134	133	132	131	129	127	35
36	140+	140+	139	137	135	134	36
37	140+	140+	140+	140+	140+	140+	37
38	140+	140+	140+	140+	140+	140+	38
	7:8	7:9	7:10	7:11	8:0	8:1	

raw score	reading age		ability scale score
	months	years & months	
1	43	3 : 7	78
2	54	4 : 6	83
3	60	5 : 0	86
4	67	5 : 7	89
5	69	5 : 9	90
6	73	6 : 1	92
7	75	6 : 3	93
8	77	6 : 5	94
9	80	6 : 8	95
10	82	6 :10	96
11	84	7 : 0	97
12	86	7 : 2	98
13	88	7 : 4	99
14	88	7 : 4	99
15	89	7 : 5	100
16	91	7 : 7	101
17	91	7 : 7	101
18	93	7 : 9	102
19	96	8 : 0	103
20	98	8 : 2	104
21	98	8 : 2	104
22	100	8 : 4	105
23	102	8 : 6	106
24	102	8 : 6	106
25	104	8 : 8	107
26	106	8 :10	108
27	106	8 :10	108
28	108	9 : 0	109
29	110	9 : 2	110
30	113	9 : 5	111
31	115	9 : 7	112
32	117	9 : 9	113
33	119	9 :11	114
34	123	10 : 3	116
35	128	10 : 8	118
36	132	11 : 0	120
37	140	11 : 8	124

Progress conversion table - Literacy Baseline to RPT1

number of completed months between Literacy Baseline and RPT1								
6 months	7 months	8 months	9 months	10 months	11 months	12 months		
progress in months	progress in months	progress in months	progress in months	progress in months	progress in months	progress in months	progress 'quotient'	percentile for progress
-16	-15	-14	-13	-12	-11	-10	70-	2-
-15	-14	-13	-12	-11	-10	-9	70	2
-14	-13	-12	-11	-10	-9	-8	71	3
-13	-12	-11	-10	-9	-8	-7	72	3
-12	-11	-10	-9	-8	-7	-6	74	4
-11	-10	-9	-8	-7	-6	-5	75	5
-10	-9	-8	-7	-6	-5	-4	77	6
-9	-8	-7	-6	-5	-4	-3	79	8
-8	-7	-6	-5	-4	-3	-2	80	9
-7	-6	-5	-4	-3	-2	-1	82	12
-6	-5	-4	-3	-2	-1	0	84	14
-5	-4	-3	-2	-1	0	1	85	16
-4	-3	-2	-1	0	1	2	86	18
-3	-2	-1	0	1	2	3	88	22
-2	-1	0	1	2	3	4	89	24
-1	0	1	2	3	4	5	91	28
0	1	2	3	4	5	6	92	30
1	2	3	4	5	6	7	94	34
2	3	4	5	6	7	8	95	37
3	4	5	6	7	8	9	96	40
4	5	6	7	8	9	10	98	45
5	6	7	8	9	10	11	99	48
6	7	8	9	10	11	12	100	50
7	8	9	10	11	12	13	102	55
8	9	10	11	12	13	14	103	58
9	10	11	12	13	14	15	105	63
10	11	12	13	14	15	16	106	66
11	12	13	14	15	16	17	107	68
12	13	14	15	16	17	18	109	72
13	14	15	16	17	18	19	111	77
14	15	16	17	18	19	20	112	78
15	16	17	18	19	20	21	114	82
16	17	18	19	20	21	22	115	84
17	18	19	20	21	22	23	116	86
18	19	20	21	22	23	24	117	87
19	20	21	22	23	24	25	119	90
20	21	22	23	24	25	26	121	92
21	22	23	24	25	26	27	122	93
22	23	24	25	26	27	28	124	94
23	24	25	26	27	28	29	125	95
24	25	26	27	28	29	30	127	96
25	26	27	28	29	30	31	129	97
26	27	28	29	30	31	32	130	98
27	28	29	30	31	32	33	130+	98+
6 months	7 months	8 months	9 months	10 months	11 months	12 months		

Progress conversion table - Literacy Baseline to RPT2

number of completed months between Literacy Baseline and RPT2

19 months	20 months	21 months	22 months	23 months	24 months	progress 'quotient'	percentile for progress
progress in months	progress in months	progress in months	progress in months	progress in months	progress in months		
-1	0	1	2	3	4	80	9
0	1	2	3	4	5	81	11
1	2	3	4	5	6	82	12
2	3	4	5	6	7	83	13
3	4	5	6	7	8	84	14
4	5	6	7	8	9	85	16
5	6	7	8	9	10	86	18
7	8	9	10	11	12	87	20
8	9	10	11	12	13	88	22
9	10	11	12	13	14	89	24
10	11	12	13	14	15	90	26
11	12	13	14	15	16	91	28
12	13	14	15	16	17	92	30
13	14	15	16	17	18	93	32
14	15	16	17	18	19	94	34
15	16	17	18	19	20	95	37
16	17	18	19	20	21	97	42
17	18	19	20	21	22	98	45
18	19	20	21	22	23	99	48
19	20	21	22	23	24	100	50
20	21	22	23	24	25	101	52
21	22	23	24	25	26	102	55
22	23	24	25	26	27	103	58
23	24	25	26	27	28	105	63
24	25	26	27	28	29	106	66
25	26	27	28	29	30	108	70
26	27	28	29	30	31	109	72
27	28	29	30	31	32	110	74
28	29	30	31	32	33	112	78
29	30	31	32	33	34	113	80
30	31	32	33	34	35	114	82
31	32	33	34	35	36	115	84
32	33	34	35	36	37	116	86
33	34	35	36	37	38	117	87
34	35	36	37	38	39	118	89
35	36	37	38	39	40	120	91
36	37	38	39	40	41	122	93
37	38	39	40	41	42	124	94
38	39	40	41	42	43	125	95
39	40	41	42	43	44	127	96
40	41	42	43	44	45	128	97
41	42	43	44	45	46	129	97
42	43	44	45	46	47	130	98
19 months	20 months	21 months	22 months	23 months	24 months		

Progress conversion table - RPT1 to RPT2

\	number of completed months between RPT1 and RPT2				
9 months	10 months	11 months	12 months		
progress in months	progress in months	progress in months	progress in months	progress 'quotient'	percentile for progress
-9	-8	-7	-6	80	9
-8	-7	-6	-5	81	11
-7	-6	-5	-4	82	12
-6	-5	-4	-3	83	13
-5	-4	-3	-2	84	14
-4	-3	-2	-1	85	16
-3	-2	-1	0	86	18
-2	-1	0	1	87	20
-1	0	1	2	88	22
0	1	2	3	89	24
1	2	3	4	91	28
2	3	4	5	92	30
3	4	5	6	93	32
4	5	6	7	94	34
5	6	7	8	95	37
6	7	8	9	96	40
7	8	9	10	98	45
8	9	10	11	99	48
9	10	11	12	100	50
10	11	12	13	101	52
11	12	13	14	102	55
12	13	14	15	103	58
13	14	15	16	104	60
14	15	16	17	105	63
15	16	17	18	106	66
16	17	18	19	108	70
17	18	19	20	109	72
18	19	20	21	110	74
19	20	21	22	112	78
20	21	22	23	113	80
21	22	23	24	114	82
22	23	24	25	115	84
23	24	25	26	117	87
24	25	26	27	118	89
25	26	27	28	119	90
26	27	28	29	120	91
27	28	29	30	121	92
28	29	30	31	122	93
29	30	31	32	123	93
30	31	32	33	124	94
31	32	33	34	125	95
32	33	34	35	126	95
33	34	35	36	127	96
34	35	36	37	128	97
35	36	37	38	129	97
36	37	38	39	130	98
9 months	10 months	11 months	12 months		

Development and standardisation

The Literacy Baseline

The Literacy Baseline was designed as a measure of those pre-literacy and initial literacy skills most commonly associated with later success in learning to read. In research studies these skills are generally assessed in a one-to-one setting, allowing for an oral response on the part of the child. It was found possible, however, to adapt such tasks to permit children to respond by underlining (or otherwise marking) a choice in a test booklet. This means that it is possible for the Literacy Baseline to be administered to groups of children (with the consequent saving in time), while still allowing individual administration where this is felt to be necessary.

The questions selected for the Literacy Baseline were drawn from a pool of 84 draft questions which were piloted in small sub-sets with groups of children. A selection of 57 questions (including practice examples) was made as a result of the piloting. These were printed in a single-booklet version of the test which was administered to a sample of 1310 children in their first year of primary education (year 1) in late September or early October 1994. These children formed the complete year groups in a national sample of 39 schools in 14 local education authorities in England and Wales. The tests were normally administered to children in small groups by their class teachers. The results of 1296 of these children were used to construct the standardised score and reading age tables on pages 36 and 37. Details of the standardisation samples for Stage 1 of the Reading Progress Test series are summarised in the table on page 47.

The participating schools were asked to arrange to further test the same sample with RPT1 in June of 1995. Results for 1056 of the children were obtained. These were used to construct the Literacy Baseline to RPT1 table on page 42.

The final published version of the Literacy Baseline consists of the questions which contributed most to its power to predict children's RPT1 scores.

In 1996, 626 of these children were tested on RPT2 and the results for these children were used to construct the Literacy Baseline to RPT2 table on page 43.

RPT1 and RPT2

RPT1 and RPT2 (together with RPT3 to RPT6) were designed to be repeated measures of the same dimension, albeit made at annual intervals. It was therefore essential that as far as possible the tests followed the same format and measured the same skills throughout. At the same time, the choice of content changes for each test to take account of developments in interest level and ability to deal with more demanding texts. To ensure comparability across the series, a common question format is used for each test.

All tests contain:

- simple single-word-based questions in which readers have to select a word according to its meaning (for most children these questions ensure a reassuring and manageable start to each test);
- questions dealing with the ability to follow a sequence of events (e.g. *who did ... ?*);
- questions requiring inference/reflection about characters and motives (*who might have said ... ?*);
- questions requiring a *true/false/doesn't say* judgement about the factual content of a passage;
- *why?* questions requiring some ability to reason about the meaning of texts;
- a cloze test of reading comprehension;
- (with the exception of Test 1) questions which require readers to read across/compare multiple texts;
- (with the exception of Test 1) more difficult reading vocabulary questions concerned with individual word meanings.

The results of development trials dictated that the actual proportion of particular question types had to vary somewhat from test to test. Also, these results meant that not all the comprehension texts trialled could be included in the final versions. For example, not all the tests contain poetry. Overall, though, the series observes a high degree of homogeneity in format, style and content.

RPT1 and RPT2 were first trialled in longer versions consisting of 47 and 58 questions respectively with samples of 298 year 1 and 303 year 2 children. As a result of these trials, versions of the final test for standardisation were assembled. RPT1 was administered to the children who had already attempted the Literacy Baseline, and RPT2 was administered to a national sample of 1120 children in 38 schools drawn from 14 local education authorities in England and Wales. In July 1996 626 of the children who took the Literacy Baseline in 1994 and RPT1 in 1995 were also tested on RPT2.

Reliability

The statistical reliability of the tests was estimated by analysing the standardisation test results to obtain internal consistency coefficients (KR20) for each test. For the Literacy Baseline the coefficient was 0.92, for RPT1 and RPT2 the values were 0.95 and 0.94, respectively. These results confirm that the tests are of an acceptable level of reliability.

Validity

The validity of the progress norms rests upon the ability of the Literacy Baseline test to predict performance on RPT1 taken 8-9 months later by the sample of 1056 children who took both tests, and on RPT2 taken 20 months later by 626 of these children.

The correlation between the Literacy Baseline and RPT1 was 0.72, that between RPT1 and RPT2 over a period of 12 months was 0.61 and that between the Literacy Baseline and RPT2 over a period of 21 months was 0.71. These are fairly high given the time intervals involved and support the validity of the tests as medium- and longer-term predictors of reading development.

	sample size	mean score	s.d.	mean age (months)	s.d.	reliability (KR20)
Literacy Baseline	1310	21.8	9.0	67.6	3.5	0.923
Reading Progress Test 1	1067	11.8	8.8	75.8	3.6	0.945
Reading Progress Test 2	1749	16.3	9.8	87.5	3.7	0.940

Table: details of standardisation samples for RPT Stage 1. (The sample size figure for RPT1 includes 11 children who undertook RPT1 but not the Literacy Baseline and that for RPT2 includes 3 children who undertook RPT2 but not the previous tests.)

It was also possible to obtain correlations between the *Reading Progress Tests* and the statutory National Curriculum tests of English, which included Reading, taken at the end of Year 2. At the time, these comprised a combination of testing and assessment procedures, including teacher assessment, each of which involved allocating children to one of four National Curriculum levels; for present purposes these were treated as a 4-point scale, which tended to *under*state the correlations.

	Reading Test	Teacher assessment of Reading
Literacy Baseline	0.50	0.66
Reading Progress Test 1	0.48	0.64
Reading Progress Test 2	0.52	0.68

These correlations support both the predictive and concurrent validity of the *Reading Progress Tests*. Generally, the correlations with the other English attainment targets, although significant, were lower, supporting the validity of the Reading measures.

Reading Progress Analysis Sheet

READING PROGRESS TESTS — STAGE ONE

Names	Date of birth d m y	Assessment 1 — Class: / Date:				Literacy baseline RPT 1 / RPT 2 — **RA1** mths	Assessment 2 — Class: / Date:				RPT 1 / RPT 2 — **RA2** mths	Progress Analysis — interval between assessments: .... months		
		Chron. age y m	Raw score	Stand. score	Reading Age y m		Chron. age y m	Raw score	Stand. score	Reading Age y m		Reading Age gain (**RA2–RA1**)	Progress quotient	Percentile

Reading Progress Tests, Stage One. Published by Hodder & Stoughton Educational. The Publishers grant permission for photocopies of this sheet to be made for use in the purchasing school only.